C000140954

On Hunger

A POETRYGRAM ANTHOLOGY

EDITED BY
HELEN COX

CONTENT DESCRIPTION

Please note that this anthology is an adult exploration of the theme of hunger. To this end, you will find poems about complicated relationships both with the self and others. You will also find, in places, explicit language and sexual references.

CONTENTS

INTRODUCTION

Hunger has been a driving force for humanity for millennia. Whether driven by the hunger for fresh meat to cook on the campfire or to realize a long-held dream, hunger, ambition and progress are inextricably linked. It can be haunting, debilitating or exhilarating.

This brief volume aims to explore the various facets of hunger, how it whittles our experience and shapes the lives we live. The hope is to provoke thought about this topic, and its social implications. To inspire discussion and raise awareness of the numerous ways in which we interact with this element of existence.

Much appreciation is extended to the poets who have contributed to this volume. All of them are followers and friends of the Poetrygram Podcast and strive (hunger?) to improve their craft with each passing week. Their work is startling, provocative and, above all else, relatable. Each piece of work subtly invites the reader into a unique space created by the poet. And in every case, vital territory is explored.

Helen Cox, Sunderland 2022.

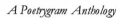

Street dog

Her mouth sinks
into garbage
and draws
out mulch.
Tongue, teeth, eyes –
all feast on it.
Years of survival
have taught her
how to track things:
trash,
traffic,
bipeds.
It's been a lifetime
of days
that arc prayerfully,
changing colour
and sound,
but ambition
has continued,
roving through intestines
and streets
in that eternal
hunt.

Suchita Parikh-Mundul

Daddy, your hands are old.

Your skin's folding into mountains
as ancient as earth. It reminds me of my childhood,
visiting ensconced towns, gazing at high peaks
and other important things you wanted me to see.
It was then I realised
your fingers aren't mine,
that they struggle to love.
But that was then, this is now.
I like to trace the gentle folds
of your hand as you sleep,
watch bone and veins
travel towards your heart.
I place my palm in your sleeping one,
reliving those mountain towns,
making fresh memories to keep.

Suchita Parikh-Mundul

Struggling up the mountain

Face taut, a rictus of concentration.
An on screen click here…
                         and …
there…
short wait in Zoom room and the
first person she sees is: herself?
old crone? Hair grey, batty, windswept?
(for Pete's sake, woman, use a comb!)

Then Betty, Barb and Ali fronting bookshelves
filled with memories, plants and plaques;
they see her – mess: dust entombed artwork
given with love, paintbrushes, books and paper.
Close friends who met each day before, carry on
now apart, with coffee and the daily catch up.

She's had to learn from scratch, instructions
on the phone, shared new skills, spread the word,
kept Barb on side: *of course, we can't give up!*
She knows its limitations: timings can be out and
 punchlines lost; but contact is maintained.

She looks out of her room to her family,
they peer at her on the screen. She's missed
 grandson's first smiles, toddler's first steps
but sees wide smiles of welcome and loving goodbyes.
She sees them grow up in front of her camera;
they watch her grow old in front of their eyes.

Helen Sadler

Cold Snap

Pink and white baby on a cold park bench with Mum
6 weeks old but 11 weeks early
blue and white brother snug in pram
6 weeks old but 11 weeks early
Made the walk to school, bottle armed, just in case
6 weeks old but 11 weeks early
back through the park, hunger wail to Mum
6 weeks old but 11 weeks early
Mum's arms, the feed and comfort all she needs
when she's 6 weeks old but 11 weeks early.

Helen Sadler

Let's Pretend

Sat with friends scoffing
lunch she mouthed eating – from her
hollow lunch box.

Source material: *The Guardian article, 'One school in Lewisham, south-east London, told the charity about a child who was "pretending to eat out of an empty lunchbox" because they did not qualify for free school meals and did not want their friends to know there was no food at home.'*

Moira Garland

An Insult To The Body

Body, owning you is like owning a dog
You want treats, you like to lie around

You didn't understand the surgery
You felt dismayed and wounded

Each painful new procedure seemed to you
a fresh denial of kindness

And now you're forced to drink a sickening squash
emptying you beyond protest

In the hours of hunger, you hear
kind voices offering biscuits to other people

behind blue curtains. You refuse
the sedative, grip tight to your right to

consciousness, travel with your tormentor
into expanding whorls of darkness

You still don't understand how you were
saved, still cringe away from touch

You like to go for walks under the trees
Gulpingly grateful for your morning tea

Clare Starling

Event Horizon

I sit before his highchair
blow on puree lumped
on a rubber spoon's tip
conduct bottom lip test

ham it up, avoid a taste.
His eyes on my level
fixed, mouth straight
absent teeth gritted.

His head exits stage left pursued
by meteor/rocket/shooting star
he strains, back arched, face
pressed against padded seat.

His hands ward off
gesture at parallel worlds
where I am weightless
sailing in the void

a silent throat-scream absence –
no use; full thrust won't propel
me clear of the black hole
sucking me back.

David Thompson

A Child With Prader-Willi Syndrome

It never stops.
An appetite that would crunch
through carcasses, sinew and bone,
whole trays of scones and entire loaves,
rainbow-grimed bacon straight from the fridge,
frozen dough, rotten compost peelings,
raw eggs. The shell.

Anything. Even boot polish, dish soap, rags,
teabags, paper scraps, the foam from headphones.
Her genetic shortfall gnawing away, spawning a need
so strong it would break
the padlock on the fridge, would eat its way
through a field of stones.

With my love, I must always
keep her hungry.

Penny Blackburn

All the Little Mothers in Hooverville

Dollies left behind someplace
they got evicted from. Somewhere back
when they had family and a mother
of their own. Now they rock somebody else's
lost baby, try to feed it with a twist of rag,
let it suck on their own emaciated finger.
In the dry reservoir bed and on the salt flats
they shut their eyes tightly.
                                    Because
when there's nothing but loss and an empty belly,
sleep won't bring answers, only quiet
the questions for a while. All the little mothers
becoming mothers-to-be, as misery finds
some fellowship in the transitory darkness,
where the gaunt and the grime don't show.
Someone, briefly, will hold them
like their memories.
                                    Like some grim
kind of wholeness. All the little mothers
becoming lost mothers because
when there isn't even enough for one
how will two survive? For a time
it will give them extra weight but only
on the inside where it doesn't make any difference,
and soon, they will whisper, just once,
an unheard prayer and take themselves
                        beyond the reach of such hunger.

Penny Blackburn

Long Hunger

Shovelling words that we gobble down, sauced with spit, spoon-fed and served up. Skin-dust flakes down, packs around us like an old snow of memory. Plastic curled raccoon-like through the hours of the night-shift. Sweet and sour loam to ward off remembered evil. Sinkholes opening into the nitrogen caverns. Slow palms, the immigrant farmer puckered along his back. The daughter, counting overtime and rest breaks on the freckles of branched fingers, bending mouths and papered muscles. 12 hours of oxygen. Knock-off proofs. Labour as a luxury, labour as a bridge. And I – standing – seated – collapsed – take orders from she who looks like me but packaged into fullness. Take down long labours for my child, funnel them, greedy, into myself. Fill myself, greedy, with owning. Look back. Bite hard. Greedy, greedy, greedy.

Penny Blackburn

Why I don't dine with Lady Grantham

My mother-in-law bossed her kitchen,
lived up to the 'Lady Grantham'
nickname from staff at Skinners,
where each Saturday she bought
only the best sausage rolls,
purplest slices of crumbly ham,
adding them to her basket of flowers
and honey from the market.

Tough as the town's Iron Lady,
the ex-hospital PA banned
intruders to her galley,
taught us patience slowly
making lunch we'd eat on trays
in a sitting room jammed with antiques
by her tall American magpie husband,
who dazzled the children with stories,
which half deaf she tried to follow,
while keeping at bay with bowls of snacks
anyone who dared venture
through her sticking, sliding door,
dismissing offers of help,
or launching a barrage of questions
that repelled the visitor,
allowing the good but inefficient
cook to elongate our hungry wait,
dispatching one thing at a time:
resting the roasted, juicy bird
before she steamed the veg,
and finally boiled the rice.

Three years on, felled by falls,
strokes and dementia, it's her turn
to wait while I boss the old lady's mouth
with soup while she's sat half asleep
after my wife, her daughter, cleaned,
clipped, then filed her mother's nails,
combed the long white-silver mane

sprouting above a cadaverous face.
I tap the spoon against the mug,
raise the broth to her protruded lips,
touching them so she, eyes shut,
knows to extend her tongue, swallow,
smile at the taste of salt oxtail.
My meal-deal sandwich lies
unopened until we leave the bare
room and warm care home
that always smells of musty food.
I dab a drop off her chin, marvel
at her hunger for life while stick thin,
a once broad-bottomed Granny
reduced to a rag doll in an arm chair,
drifting on childhood reverie,
gossiping about, and with, her parents.

I remember how she wailed
to be let back home at her first Christmas
in the lodge, when for a trial
we went for a buffet at the hotel,
loaded our plates and watched
her pick at mince pies, olives and ham,
pretending it was fun to hear
two crooners sing 'Let It Snow',
until after in the cab she blew
a blizzard of rage, booming,
'You can't treat people like this!'
Leaving everyone in the people carrier
frozen with shock, I wheeled
her into the building she despised,
navigated her chair on to the lift,
rolling down the corridor
past nosy residents and parked
her in the room to find
she at least had forgotten
the uproar. And that's why I don't eat
with my mother-in-law anymore.

Gavin Lumsden

Urban Badger

Trash cans clag up along the roadside,
pavements crazed and busy with ants.
We sit, hushed in the back of the van,
waiting for the traffic-light change –
watching a Badger, unfazed by the city fug;
hauling a damp cube of take-out styrene
then snouting away pigeons come for an easy meal.
The Badger has a day-gait, its back leg jiving out
bevelling from the hip and bilgy fur,
a snout full of ill-healed welts.
Pigeons peck and clamour -
such a messy eater, quickly scarfing down scraps
then shrugging off, away into a hedge
leaving the pigeons scolding as light flickers green.

Zoë Sîobhan Howarth-Lowe

Physics Paper Found Folded Beneath the Leg of a Stool in the Ground Floor Laboratory.

1. Title

The effects of resistance towards
high-volume women who dare
to wear Technicolour clothing.

2. Introduction

Traditionally, high-volume women have been shamed
into wearing dark shades. Simulating uncontainable
dark matter, or a black hole or a shadow that disappears,
as though it was never there, under the hard stare
of the Moon.

Resistance to such individuals expressing
the quantum palette of their identity
has been spearheaded by beauty magazine editors
who assert women with breasts big as twin-Jupiters
and waistlines that might,

at the speed of light, take more than a lifetime
to circumnavigate, should jettison colours and carbs
in favour of spaghettification. These doctrines
were internalised by the general female population
who, in the ladies' toilets,

applied purple lipstick advertised in the magazines
they read, pausing only to recite the practiced lie
to their friends, who had unwittingly asked
for advice on how to dress: *black will always be
the new thin*, they said.

3. Aim

The aim of the experiment is to test
the real-world implications of resistance
towards high-volume women who dance
with every tone on the spectrum,
as if it were their birth right,
reflecting unfiltered light
into narrow eyes.

4. Hypothesis

The misogynistic policing
of normal female body types
(sometimes by women themselves)
is creating a rainbow shortage.

5. Risk Assessment

People with a BMI between 18 and 25 may find women who fit
a non-standard model more visible for the duration of this experiment,
and be forced to consider new ideas
such as:

    a.   High-volume women deserve to be seen.

    b.   It is inappropriate to disguise disgust
          for high-volume women with counterfeit concern
          while issuing unsolicited lifestyle advice torn
          from pages of the very publications
          that have launched a hate campaign
          against such women.

6. Method
6a. Materials

- 1 million tears cried by a high-volume woman
  over a period of 40 years
  in which fat-shaming asteroids
  impacted deep in the playground /
  workplace / doctor's office / street.

- 51,881.8 x 1250ml beakers
  (to contain the teardrops).

- 4 decades of accumulated rage
  fuelled by job offers denied
  to the participant
  because she was *fat*
  heated to the surface temperature of the sun
  (6000° Kelvin).

- A plus-size jumpsuit sewn
  of upcycled nylon, harvested
  from a retired hot air balloon.

- A red silk thong
  too big to be sold
  on the high street.

- A gravity-defying
  spray-on bra
  in electric blue
  that won't stab
  into underboob.

- A pair of
  Saturn-yellow
  heels. So high,
  the air thins.

6b. Steps

1. The tears and the anger
    were easily extracted
    from the participant.

2. The two substances were combined
    and a rudimentary rainbow formed
    in a laboratory setting
    to demonstrate that 4 decades lost
    in a void hadn't disintegrated
    every future choice.

3. The participant was encouraged to try
    on the plus-size thong, the sky-high shoes,
    the friction-free bra and the jumpsuit
    that had kissed the stars.

4. Someone outside the laboratory
    shouted in through an open window:
    You shouldn't be flaunting
    such an unhealthy body.
    People might be encouraged to copy.

    We closed the window.

5. The participant was released
    back into their natural habitat.

6c. Diagram

We stare
lovingly through tele-
scopes at the faces of far-off
planets, round as doughnut holes.
Documenting their beauty on official
databases. Yet choose to chide those
globular bodies orbiting closest to our
own. Judging density, needlessly, even
though it is well within the bounds
of possibility they might, by some
measures, be considered
h e a v e n l y .

7. Results

- The participant did not look thin.

- Her smile bore greater resemblance to a rainbow.

- She reported a 94% reduction
  in the number of fucks she gave
  when people asked her
  if she'd tried losing weight
  by eating 57.6g of grapes
  whenever she felt hungry.

- She was told by one passer-by
  (a 92-year-old woman sporting a tangerine hair rinse)
  that she had brightened her day.

8. Discussion

8a. Trends

There was a positive correlation
between wearing vibrant colour combinations
and the realisation that shadows are no place
for any sentient creature to live.

8b. Scientific Explanation

We concluded this was because the participant felt
the colours more accurately represented their authentic self.

8c. Validation

It is better to stand naked
before the looking glass
and smile at the buxom woman
staring back
than to use the eyes of another
as a mirror.

9. Conclusion

Earth is being denied rainbows
on a daily basis
due to resistance
towards those women
who eat three square meals a day
and aren't ashamed to take up space.

Helen Cox

Mark Me with Lipstick Kisses

Mark me with lipstick kisses
Stain my collar with Relentlessly Red
Or Ruby Woo
Bruise my skin with vivid shades
Brand me as yours

Mark me with lipstick kisses
Smear my cheek with Daddy's Girl
Or Fusion Pink
Colour my neck with Lasting Passion
My chest with Punch Drunk Love

Mark me with lipstick kisses
And I will never wipe them away…

Andrew Douglas

The Sound of Her Voice

Louisiana sunset sultry and warm
Honeyed Bourbon words flow
And dare a man to dream
Yet threaten heartbreak

An artist struck blind
Would not mourn his loss
With words of comfort from her lips
Echoing across his heart
And filling the void in his soul

Andrew Douglas

Solanum Dulcamara

Bittersweet vines crawl from my lungs,
constricting my throat, playing a stutter
on my vocal cords, only to croak
purple flowers in my mouth.

A witches' protection and curse is my

silence.

Red are the berries that cluster my words. Eat
the rhyme with the rhythm of secrets. Hide
the strength of who I am, who I was and who
I could be.

Jennifer Duffy

Living the Dream

I eat the crumbs and spilled oats from the cupboards
the last potato with more eyes than a spider,
baked on the wood from our remaining shelf.
I will have to forage, hunt and fish soon,
or break into the houses of the dead.
I'm not cut out for this survival thing
yet I'm still here, for whatever that's worth.
I never saw myself as one of those
blessed with the instincts, will and cunning
to make it into dark loneliness,
which stretches on longer than death,
and I'm pretty sure I'll never fall in love again.
But my ghosts are with me when I fall asleep
so I guess I'll keep on breathing for them.

Mark Connors

Wormhole

The internet enthrals me,
> just like a hungry bird
>> I tap
> for it to feed me

and swallow
> every
>> word.

I only have to see the screen,
> my mind just
>> disappears
> into the flashing images
>> it snatches me

and steers.
Because I saw one video
> I'm urged to see

one more,
> before I know it

I'm caught up
> and dragged
>> from store to store.

There never was this catnip
> back when we just had books,

now every look's

incentivised
> baited

with juicy hooks.
I know it's an addiction -
    this worm should really turn,
but when my 'phone is calling
    into the net
        I squirm.

Sharron Green

Things I Missed Eating in Lockdown

Garlic prawns in Barcelona.
Cream tea by a Cornish bay.
Bratwurst in a German garden.
Haggis made for Hogmanay.

Five-cheese toastie after spin class.
Gelato in a Tuscan square.
Birthday cake with bubbly girlfriends.
Candy floss at the county fair.

Listing dishes, lockdown misses,
makes me queasy with delight,
all those calories forsaken
so – why are my jeans still tight?

Sharron Green

Black Hole

The fuel runs out and
I implode –
silently.

I eat my way
out of myself:
crack atoms;
gnaw for molecule
marrow;
dribble plasma.

In space, no
one can
hear you
slurp.

I bloat with
nothingness
as my body
teaches itself
how not to be –
a darkling orb,
sucking down
the light itself.

Beyond the
event horizon,
there is nothing
to do
but
eat.

Nicholas Rooney

Snap

That sleeking brown crocodile sneaked into my dreams last night,
the same one that took Mr Wright's hands right off
when we were children. That
left me trembling under the sheets
for weeks.

Mr Wright with his plastic claws forever reaching.

That same beast that snap snap snap chases our kids
through colourful jungling pages, that snap snap snap
whips them to a squall around
the breakfast table. Unsettling
cups and bowls.

This night it came for you my love. I noticed
you didn't put up much of a fight.
I couldn't help but blame you
for playing dead, star-fished out flat:
for being so much
bloody meat.

Jennie E. Owen

Biographies

Penny Blackburn has appeared in many journals and anthologies both online and in print, including *Riggwelter, IS&T, The High Window* and *Poetry Society News*. She was awarded 2nd place in the Ver poetry competition 2022 and her debut collection will be available from Yaffle in Spring 2023.

Mark Connors is a poet, novelist, creative writing facilitator and managing editor at YAFFLE Press. His debut poetry pamphlet, *Life is a Long Song* was published by OWF Press in 2015. His first full length collection, *Nothing is Meant to be Broken* was published by Stairwell Books in 2017. His second poetry collection, *Optics*, was published in 2019. His third collection, *After*, was published in 2021. A joint collection with his YAFFLE colleagues, *Reel Bradford* was published in association with Bradford City of Film in 2019. Mark is currently working on a hybrid book of fiction, non-fiction, travel writing and poetry, due out in 2022.

Helen Cox is a poet and novelist from the North East of England. Her first pamphlet, *Water Signs* was released in 2018, followed by her second pamphlet *Where Concrete and Coral Bells Kiss* in 2019. Helen has just released her first full-length poetry collection, *Stiletto Feminism for Beginners*. She teaches an annual poetry masterclass at Keats House and a selective poetry masterclass online each autumn. More information can be found at helencoxbooks.com

Jennifer Duffy is a writer based in Edinburgh, Scotland. Graduating this year with a first class BA (Honours) in English literature at The Open University, she is currently creating her first poetry pamphlet. Inspired by poisonous plants, her work aims to explore themes of mental illness, neurodiversity and witchcraft. When she isn't writing, Jennifer can be found reading fantasy novels and tarot cards. She, also, owns Bewitching Fates; a small business which offers tarot readings.

Andrew Douglas was raised in the North Midlands and has never strayed far from his roots. Until recently he had never strayed far from his lifelong passion for photography either but years of exposure to Radio 4 and an interest in words and their meanings (not to mention a lot of encouragement) has led him to experiment with writing as a creative outlet.

Moira Garland is a Leeds-based poet and short fiction writer. She won the Leeds Peace Poetry Competition (2016), and the Poised Pen competition (2015). She was highly commended in the YorkMix Poems For Children Competition (2021), and commended in others. Her poetry appeared on the Wakefield *Moonriver* (2019) celebrating the 1969 moon landing, in numerous anthologies, and in magazines such as *The North, Stand, The Adriatic, Consilience, Fragmented Voices,* and *Sarasvati*. A poem was set to music by Freya Ireland as part of the Leeds Lieder Festival (2019).

Sharron Green is a 'poet of a certain age' whose writing blends nostalgia, comments on modern life and odes to nature. She enjoys experimenting with rhymes and poetic forms.

Sharron has published *Introducing Rhymes_n_Roses* and *Viral Odes* and has contributed to over ten international anthologies including the Poetrygram Annual 2020.

In 2021 she studied for an MA in Creative Writing at the University of Surrey where she assisted with the Surrey New Writers Festival and in 2022 completed the Helen Cox Poetry Masterclass.

Sharron regularly performs her work and facilitates poetry workshops.

Zoë Sîobhan Howarth-Lowe is a Poet and Mum from Dukinfield. She has an MA in Poetry from Bath Spa University. Her first pamphlet *'Love is the way bark grows'* came out with Half Moon Books in June 2019 and her second *'I have grown two hearts'* with Hedgehog Press in Autumn 2020. Her First Collection *'Pocket Full of Stones'* was published by Indigo Dreams in 2021. Her work has appeared in Anthologies and Journals including *For the Silent, Atrium, Ink, Sweat and Tears, Picaroon, Algebra of*

Owls, Magma and *Here Comes Everyone.* Twitter: @ZSHowarthLowe
Website: www.zshowarthlowe.com

Gavin Lumsden lives in North London and has been writing poetry for five years. He has had poems published in *Cake* and *Wildfire* and was long-listed on the Briefly Write prize this year.

Jennie E. Owen's writing has been widely published online, in literary journals and anthologies. She teaches Creative Writing for The Open University and lives in Lancashire, UK with her husband and three children. She is currently working towards her PhD with Manchester Metropolitan University.

Suchita Parikh-Mundul is a freelance writer, copy editor and poet. Some of her articles can be read at *The Swaddle.* Her poems have been featured in several literary magazines, including *Parcham, Yugen Quest Review, The Bombay Literary Magazine, Outlook India, Muse India,* and Sahitya Akademi's *Indian Literature.* Her work has also been included in anthologies like *The Well-Earned* (ed. Kiriti Sengupta, Hawakal, 2022), *Wuxing Lyrical: Playful Poems Based on Chinese Astrology* (ed. Rhys Hughes, 2022), and other international compilations. She lives in Mumbai, India.

Nicholas Rooney grew up in Liverpool and currently lives in South-East London. He started writing angst-ridden poetry as a teenager and hasn't got round to stopping yet. He has previously been published in *Inkapture* online magazine and *Gold Dust Magazine.*

For the last few years, he has been working on a small pamphlet focusing on the subject of "divinity". He is also putting together an interactive online experience aimed at exploring London through the words of various writers from history. For the latest information on Nicholas's work, please visit: nicholas-rooney-poetry.co.uk.

Helen Sadler was brought up by the sea and now reluctantly lives almost as far from the coast as possible. She misses the sea but finds some consolation in the canal network of the East Midlands which appeared in the anthology *Where We Live* which she published in 2022 as part of a women's collective. She started writing poetry nearly fifty years ago as a student, then took a long break before starting again in the 2020s. More information about *Where We Live* is available through Villageverse2022@gmail.com Her poetry was kindly included in the First Poetrygram Annual in 2020.

Clare Starling started writing poetry during lockdown, after leaving a role in public policy to support her son when he was diagnosed with autism. Her poems have since appeared in *Sentinel Literary Quarterly*, *Erbacce*, and *Frosted Fire's Wildfire Words*, and were recognised in *Rialto* and AUB competitions. She survived cancer in her thirties, and her poetry explores how the body, the mind, and our complicated social existences influence our daily experiences of pain and beauty.

David Thompson practises law by day and fatherhood by night. In poetry, he has mastered the share screen function on Zoom. His work has featured in magazines and anthologies such as *Atrium, Magma, Orbis* and *New Contexts 3* (Coverstory Books, 2022).

For more information about the Poetrygram Podcast, please visit helencoxbooks.com.

If you enjoyed this anthology, please leave a review to support the poets who created it.

Lightning Source UK Ltd.
Milton Keynes UK
UKHW040313160223
417041UK00004B/64